Love NOTES for DAD

Love
NOTES
for
DAD

New Leaf Press

First printing: March 2002

Copyright © 2002 by New Leaf Press, Inc. All rights reserved. No part of this book may be used or reproduced in any manner whatsoever without written permission of the publisher, except in the case of brief quotations in articles and reviews. For information write: New Leaf Press, Inc., P.O. Box 726, Green Forest, AR 72638.

ISBN: 0-89221-524-0
Library of Congress Number: 2001098914

Printed in the United States of America

Please visit our website for other great titles:
www.newleafpress.net

⏤ A SPECIAL NOTE ⏤

This book is a gift of stories and
also a special remembrance of what
you've meant to your own. Stories are a
connection, a bridge, for humans. All of us
live and love. We have awareness. The
relationships formed from our unique
traits are always with us.

So enjoy these memories, and
think of the ones you've made with your
children. Read the note from them that
follows, and know that you are
loved very much.

Dear DAD,

Love,

DAD

CHAPTER ONE

WE STAND BY YOU

THE FOLLOWING IS AN EXCERPT FROM
AN E-MAIL SENT HOME BY ONE OF THE
OFFICERS ABOARD THE USS *WINSTON S.
CHURCHILL* IN THE DAYS FOLLOWING THE
TERRORIST ATTACKS OF SEPTEMBER 11,
2001. IT WAS POSTED TO THE U.S.
NAVY WEBSITE, AND MOVES US TO
UNDERSTAND THAT AMERICA IS STILL
STRONG, AND STILL HAS THE RESPECT
AND SUPPORT OF MANY NATIONS.

Dear Dad,

We have seen the articles and the photographs
[of the attacks], and they are sickening. Being isolated
as we are, I don't think we appreciate the full scope of

what is happening back home, but we are definitely feeling the effects.

About two hours ago the junior officers were called to the bridge to conduct ship-handling drills. We were about to do a "man overboard" when we got a call from *Lutjens (D 185)*, a German warship that was moored ahead of us on the pier in Plymouth, England.

While in port, *Winston S. Churchill* and *Lutjens* got together for a sports day/cookout on our fantail, and we made some pretty good friends. Now at sea they called over on bridge-to-bridge, requesting to pass us close up on our port side, to say goodbye. We prepared to render them honors on the bridge wing, and the captain told the crew to come topside to wish them farewell.

As they were making their approach, our conning officer ... announced that they were flying an American flag. As they came even closer, we saw that it was flying at half-mast. The bridge wing was crowded

Then spake the Lord to Paul in the night by a vision, Be not afraid, but speak, and hold not thy peace: For I am with thee, and no man shall set on thee to hurt thee: for I have much people in this city (Acts 18:9–10).

with people as the boatswain's mate blew two whistles — "attention to port."

Lutjens came up alongside and we saw that the entire crew of the German ship were manning the rails, in their dress blues. They had made up a sign that was displayed on the side that read "We Stand By You." Needless to say there was not a dry eye on the bridge as they stayed alongside us for a few minutes and we cut our salutes. It was probably the most powerful thing I have seen in my entire life and more than a few of us fought to retain our composure.

It was a beautiful day outside today. We are no longer at liberty to divulge over unsecure e-mail our location, but we could not have asked for a finer day at sea. The German navy did an incredible thing for this crew, and it has truly been the highest point in the days since the attacks. It's amazing to think that only a half-century ago things were quite different, and to see the unity that is being demonstrated throughout

Europe and the world makes us all feel proud to be out here doing our job.

After [*Lutjens*] pulled away and we prepared to begin our man-overboard drills, the officer of the deck turned to me and said, "I'm staying Navy."

> ## THE FATHER'S MOST IMPORTANT RESPONSIBILITY IS TO COMMUNICATE THE REAL MEANING OF CHRISTIANITY TO HIS CHILDREN.
> — JAMES C. DOBSON

Then spake the Lord to Paul in the night by a vision, Be not afraid, but speak, and hold not thy peace: For I am with thee, and no man shall set on thee to hurt thee: for I have much people in this city (Acts 18:9–10).

DAD

CHAPTER TWO

"FOR REAL" DAD

JULIE TURNER

IT DOESN'T TAKE A WHOLE LOT OF FUEL
TO REKINDLE A RELATIONSHIP — EVEN
ONE THAT DIED OUT ALMOST 40 YEARS
AGO. BOTH PARTIES MUST BE WILLING TO
MAKE RECONCILIATION, BUT SOMEONE
STILL HAS TO MAKE THE FIRST MOVE. IT
HAS OFTEN BEEN SAID, "IF YOU
COMMAND YOUR ACTIONS, YOUR
FEELINGS WILL FOLLOW." LIFE IS TOO
SHORT TO HARBOR BITTER FEELINGS.
MAYBE IT'S TIME TO TAKE THAT FIRST
STEP TOWARD HEALING AND
RESTORATION.

He was only 44. Who would have thought his life would end so soon? My brother was a tall, handsome, very intelligent man. I doubt if I could ever meet a more impeccable character. Floyd loved to ride his motorcycle and was a very cautious driver. Everything had to be in perfect order before taking off for a ride — right down to situating the zipper on his riding jacket to exactly the right position (and checking it again). He'd maneuvered that same curve on his motorcycle a hundred times but just one fatal slip on that dreary October night and he was gone.

I absolutely dreaded the thought of calling my father, but he had to know that Floyd had died. (After all, Floyd was his first-born child.) My father. I didn't even know my father. I had had no real contact with him since I had been a toddler.

All of my life, I had thought about my father — what he was like, what he did from day to day, who he really was, and why he had never contacted me. All I knew about him was what my mother had told me

Behold, how good and how pleasant it is for brethren to dwell together in unity! (Ps. 133:1).

(which wasn't much). He was an air force staff sergeant stationed on the island of Okinawa when I was born. Once in a great while I'd look through the old black and white photographs that my father had developed from those Okinawa days when I was an infant — that pristine family portrait of my brother, my sister, and me with Mom and Dad behind us. We looked like such a happy family. We looked like we belonged to each other. There's that picture of my father lying on a peculiar-looking tree branch. He was so handsome. There's the one of him wearing his scuba-diving equipment getting ready to plunge into the ocean, and those other pictures that captured him doing things that made him look either fun-loving or intelligent. And what a great photographer he was!

I was too young to remember anything about Okinawa. After we all grew up, Floyd admitted that when he was a mischievous five year old, he set a field of elephant grass on fire on the island. I was told that my mom's transportation to the hospital to deliver me was the back of a motorcycle. Those days on Okinawa must have been very happy times for all of us!

Soon after my family returned to the United States, my parents divorced. My mother remarried right away and I never understood what happened with my father. Mom's second husband became abusive toward us children. We called him by his first name. I didn't even want to refer to him as my step-dad and called him "Mom's husband."

On those rare occasions when my father would come up in conversations, I would refer to him as my "real dad" although I hadn't seen him in so many years. There was one brief attempt at reconciliation after I graduated high school, but it ended in failure. Too much pain.

It wasn't until 20 years later that I managed to muster up enough nerve to contact him again. I wanted to find out how he would feel about meeting his grandchildren, Jacob and Heather, since we were going to be vacationing in his area of the country and

Behold, how good and how pleasant it is for brethren to dwell together in unity! (Ps. 133:1).

DAD

would be traveling close to the town where he lived. I was excitedly planning out a spring vacation with my children on that cold winter day.

It was the most difficult phone call I had ever made up to that time. I almost lost my nerve but then a sense of boldness came over me and I dialed the phone. There was a long pause when I told him who I was. Feeling very uneasy, I finally just said, "You don't sound like you want to talk."

"No, I don't," was his reply. Another failure. I didn't even get to mention why I was calling. At first I felt like I just didn't want to ever think about him again if I could help it, but then later I decided to begin praying regularly that God would soften my dad's heart toward me.

It was just nine months later when I had to call him about Floyd's accident. After the past two failures, I did not want to talk to him again. But, yes I did. The truth is that I yearned to talk to him, but I didn't want to be rejected and have those hurtful feelings all over again. I felt an uneasy queasiness and butterflies in my stomach as I picked up the receiver and began to dial his number. I bit my lip as the call went through and began to ring in my ear. "Hello?"

I paused for a moment, and almost stammered. "This is Julie. I thought you should know that something has happened to Floyd."

I began to explain to him about Floyd's accident, and when it was his time to speak, he actually seemed to care. There was intense sadness in his voice.

After we had talked about Floyd, *he continued to talk.* This was not the icy, cold man of the last phone call. Instead of being aloof, he began to share stories about my childhood. It was a long, enlightening conversation. I found out that when I was a toddler, he was my favorite thing in the world. I was his little pet and would crawl up in his lap. He remembered when I was sitting under the plum tree in the backyard and had eaten so many plums that I got sick and he came out after me. He told me that losing his family had been the saddest thing in his life.

Behold, how good and how pleasant it is for brethren to dwell together in unity! (Ps. 133:1).

DAD

After that phone call it seemed to me that a perfectly good daddy had been exchanged for a poor substitute. What would it have been like to have a *real dad* who cared about me while I was growing up?

We exchanged e-mail addresses, and on the day of Floyd's funeral, I received an e-mail from my father. He told me that the day of the funeral was the saddest day of his life and that it would take a long, long time for him to get over Floyd's death.

I saw that softer, sentimental side of him more clearly when he sent me a timeworn photo album he'd saved for over 40 years. He didn't want me to feel badly about the album not having any pictures of me in it and explained that I hadn't been born yet when it was put together.

We've been keeping in touch regularly now and he plans to come to my area of the country for a visit soon. How curious life is. So many years, so much silence between us. Yet, the very day I had set aside to take time for journaling our budding relationship, I received a real letter in the mail from him — the first one in my life. He offered help and fatherly advice in an important endeavor that I had mentioned to him earlier. I could never have imagined anything like that coming from my true flesh-and-blood dad. Indeed, God did soften his heart toward me. Incredibly, on the same day that I received the letter, I found an e-mail from my father that I thought I had lost. In the midst of 50 or more titles on my computer screen, my eyes fell right on the title "For Real Dad." I was overcome with excitement as I re-read his response to a previous e-mail of mine:

> You can introduce me to anyone you want any time. This is a misunderstanding that is the result of 38 lost years . . . .I have given you the impression that I am a hard person to get to know and you are worried that I don't want to know any of your friends. The truth is, I need to know your friends and you need to introduce me as your father, which is

Behold, how good and how pleasant it is for brethren to dwell together in unity! (Ps. 133:1).

something undreamed of a few months ago.
So let's keep trying and I am sure that
misunderstandings will forever be with us as
with all people.

You and I both know that this getting
acquainted is extremely important and is the
result of your initiative. If it wasn't for you, and
your initiative, none of this would have
happened. We are both very lucky for this
chance, and let's keep going, mistakes and all. A
few months ago you would never have
dreamed that you could introduce your real
dad to your friends, and I am not going to
destroy that for you. Also, a few months ago I
could not have dreamed of getting acquainted
with a "for real" family. Let's keep this very
important thing going.

Your dad and the grandfather of Jacob and
Heather. For real.

IF I HAD MY CHILD TO RAISE OVER AGAIN,
I'd build self-esteem first,
    and the house later.
I'd finger-paint more,
    and point the finger less.
I would do less correcting
    and more connecting.
I'd take my eyes off my watch,
    and watch with my eyes.
I'd take more hikes
    and fly more kites.
I'd stop playing serious,
    and seriously play.
I would run through more fields
    and gaze at more stars.
I'd do more hugging
    and less tugging.

— Diane Loomans
from "If I Had My Child
to Raise Over Again"

Behold, how good and how pleasant it is for brethren to dwell together in unity! (Ps. 133:1).

DAD

CHAPTER THREE

IT'S WHO YOU KNOW

SOMETIMES, KNOWING THE RIGHT PERSON AT THE RIGHT TIME WILL GIVE US AN ADVANTAGE IN LIFE. ACCESS TO A CERTAIN SCHOOL, AN EMPLOYMENT OPPORTUNITY, OR A FANTASTIC BUSINESS DEAL MAY COME ABOUT BECAUSE OF A SPECIAL ACQUAINTANCE. THERE IS, HOWEVER, ONLY ONE RELATIONSHIP THAT IS REQUIRED OF US HERE. IF WE HAVE THAT CONNECTION WITH THE HEAVENLY FATHER, WE NEED NOT WORRY FOR ANYTHING — HE HAS PROMISED TO TAKE CARE OF ALL OF OUR NEEDS. THERE IS ONLY ONE WAY TO ACCESS HIM. TO KNOW THE FATHER FIRST REQUIRES THAT WE KNOW HIS SON.

During the Civil War, a young soldier walking over a battlefield came across a dear friend who was shot. His life was draining rapidly away. The soldier straightened out the shattered limb, washed the blood from his fallen comrade's face, and made him as comfortable as possible under difficult circumstances. He then said he would stay with his friend as long as life was still there. Then he asked if there was anything more he might do.

"Yes," replied the dying soldier, "if you have a piece of paper, I will dictate a note to my father, and I think I can still sign it. My father is a prominent judge in the North, and if you take him this message, he will help you." The note read:

Dear Father,

I am dying on the battlefield; one of my best friends is helping me and has done his best for me. If he ever comes to you, be kind to him for your son Charlie's sake.

Jesus answered . . . if ye had known me, ye should have known my Father also (John 8:19).

DAD

Then with rapidly stiffening fingers, he signed his name. After the war, the young soldier in ragged uniform sought out the prominent judge. The servants refused to admit him because he looked like the many other tramps coming by for handouts.

He made a ruckus and insisted he see the judge. Finally, hearing the commotion, the judge came out and read the note. He at first was convinced it was another beggar's appeal. But he studied the signature, and even in its scribbled state, he recognized it as his own son's.

He embraced the soldier, led him into his home, and said, with tears coursing down his cheeks, "You can have anything that my money can buy, and everything that my influence can secure."

What brought about the sudden change in the judge's attitude? It was the signature of his son Charlie affixed to the bottom of that note. It was the father-son relationship that made the difference.

There is an old saying in our world: "It's not *what*

you know, it's *who* you know, that counts!"

That same principle holds true in the spiritual realm. All the knowledge in the world will not help you as you approach your Heavenly Father, but your personal relationship with Jesus Christ, the Son, will open to you all kinds of possibilities! It's not too late to make right that relationship with the Son, who will in turn provide you an access to the throne room of heaven!!

Jesus answered . . . if ye had known me, ye should have known my Father also (John 8:19).

DAD

CHAPTER FOUR

SOONER OR LATER

THE KNOWLESES ARE PRIME EXAMPLES
OF THE PIONEER SPIRIT OF MORE THAN
A CENTURY AGO — OKLAHOMANS
WHO ARE HARD WORKERS AND FAMILY
ORIENTED. THE STORY YOU'RE ABOUT
TO READ IS A PRIME EXAMPLE OF WHAT
CAN HAPPEN WHEN A FATHER IS
TENACIOUS IN HIS PRAYERS. IT'S THE
STORY OF A FATHER — AND A MOTHER —
WHO STARTED AND FINISHED A CRUCIAL
RACE, AND STAKED THEIR CLAIM TO A
HEAVENLY HOMESTEAD.

One fine morning in 1889, a rag-tag group of hopeful settlers lined up on the prairie in northern Indian Territory. Families in wagons, men on horseback, some on foot — all tensed as they awaited the signal that would allow them to race for their own stake. The famous "Land Run of 1889" was about to commence. Wherever a person stopped and staked out land was where the family homestead would be established.

Finally, a shot was heard and riders, runners, and "fast walkers" rumbled over the prairie. It would be almost two decades before the area would be designated for statehood, but this "pre-Oklahoma" would become the defining event for subsequent generations of folks with the pioneering spirit.

Naturally, pioneers like these with the pluck to plant themselves on the prairie were no ordinary settlers. Life in that climate was difficult at best, but they were free to make their own choices, to make their own way. They became known as "sooners," folks who were determined to find a fetching spot of land

Delight thyself also in the LORD; and he shall give thee the desires of thine heart (Ps. 37:4).

sooner than anyone else. The tag stuck, along with that adventurous, independent spirit.

Along with hard work came a renewed sense for prayer among the people in this rough land. Pioneer mothers who lived in sod houses and worked themselves literally to death wanted a better life for their children. That internal ethic is still alive and well in this thriving state today.

Judd was a young man who was long on charm but short on spiritual strength. Carol, however, had grown up in a Christian home and enjoyed her life. She met and fell in love with Judd, who had the ability to provide well for a family. He was widely liked, and life would almost certainly be fun with him.

They married. Raised a family. Settled into the American dream. Now, by Judd's own admission, he took his bride far away from Christ. She followed his lead and began living "the good life," you know, the one the world tells us is preferable to the freedom found in Christ. Not surprisingly, the children with whom Judd and Carol were blessed decided that if this life was good enough for Mom and Dad, it was good enough for them. They indulged in drinking, partying — activities that certainly didn't include church attendance.

They continued to live the "good life" until the day in 1986 when Judd Knowles found Christ. His story isn't unlike others, but for people who know Judd, the transformation continues to be dramatic, even after all these years.

Having resisted surrendering to the Christian life, Judd became one of those people who make a complete turnaround and started walking a different path; he literally repented of his past life. Better yet, Carol walked along with him. Returning to the faith of her youth, she embarked on a whole new adventure in her marriage. There was only one problem: the kids.

Maybe that religious stuff is all well and good for Mom and Dad, they reasoned, *but don't bother us with it.*

The anguish that Judd and Carol felt is

Delight thyself also in the LORD; and he shall give thee the desires of thine heart (Ps. 37:4).

DAD

understandable only to parents who have had similar experiences. They wanted their children's conversions *yesterday*. The toughest hide to penetrate was Robert. "Robbie" was a typical American man: tough, solid, and well-liked. Just don't crowd around him with that Jesus stuff. *That's for weak people*, he thought. Weak is not the image the modern man wants to project.

The prayers of two parents continued, however. Morning, noon, and night. For years.

As with so many others, the horrific events of September 11, 2001, prompted some introspection. Young Robert Knowles was one of those. Knowing that his parents were passionate about his attending a certain Christian retreat weekend for men, he shocked his father one day by phoning and saying he'd like to go.

At the retreat, Robert came to the realization that just attending the weekend — big step though it was — wouldn't bring him to the peace he secretly desired, but he was willing and had an open heart to listen to the speakers, take part in the discussions, and talk to God in private moments. As he yielded himself to the events and the beckoning of the Holy Spirit, something began to happen. As Robert tells it:

You probably don't know me, but I have an exciting true-life story to tell you.

About a month ago you became my brother or sister. You see, September 20, 2001, I went on a Christian retreat weekend. I thought I wanted to find out if there was really something to getting saved and having God in my life. Well, I made it through the first evening and I had learned a few of the names of the people, but I didn't feel any different.

Then God started working on me and I started understanding the stories I was listening to from the speakers, and I was being touched.

Now listen, keep in mind I run a dozer for a living and I have a kind of "tough guy" image to hold up. I wasn't about to let

Delight thyself also in the LORD; and he shall give thee the desires of thine heart (Ps. 37:4).

anyone see me cry. I would rather die.

I have been shy all my life. From the time I was little, if I had to get on stage in front of a lot of people . . . you could forget about getting me to do anything except sweat, shake, and forget what I was supposed to say or do.

Well, Friday evening I'm sitting at my table, with three other people I barely know. We were discussing what the last speaker was talking about. All of a sudden, another person that was on the retreat asked the two table leaders and me to go to the chapel and pray for him. I had never prayed with any seriousness, so I was thinking maybe someone from one of the other tables might go pray for him. Then my new friend and table leader grabbed my hand, got up, and said, "Let's go to the chapel." Somehow I went with them. When we got to the chapel, my table leader arranged four chairs in a circle and we took hands, then sat down. Butch said Bill would start the prayer; one at a time then to him, then me, then Joel, the fellow that needed prayer. Well, when it came my turn, I clammed up so they skipped me and Joel prayed for himself. While he was praying, God was working on me and it was really bothering me that I didn't at least try to pray for him. When he finished, it was supposed to go back to Bill but no one said a word. Then something gave me a push and I started praying — first for Steve, then for me. I humbled myself for the first time and I asked Jesus to come into my heart and soul and to forgive me for all the sins I had committed in my life. I cried.

Later that night I went back to my room and talked to my roommate about what happened. I told him I thought I might have been touched by God. He said, "If you died tomorrow do you think you would go to

Delight thyself also in the LORD; and he shall give thee the desires of thine heart (Ps. 37:4).

heaven?" I told him I didn't think I would. He counseled me.

I went to sleep and the next morning we all went to the chapel for communion. That's where you get up and tell people the bad things you want out of your life and for Jesus to help you. For some reason, I wasn't even nervous — for the first time in my life. I knew exactly what I was going to say. I had decided to give my life to Christ. So when it came my turn I went to the front, picked up my little cup of wine, turned to the congregation and said: "I want to thank everyone for touching my heart with their stories." Then I started to spill my guts! I guess Jesus already knew what I was going to say. He let me tell everyone else, with emotion, and I just bawled. One hour later, I told Butch I thought I got saved because everyone seemed different. They all seemed to be my brothers and sisters. I wanted to hug them all. Butch, Bill, Joel, and I held hands and I told everyone I had committed my life to Christ and Jesus had forgiven me.

Let me tell you, I'm not shy anymore; Jesus took that away! My life has had a complete change. I have been reborn. I sing in front of my church (solo) and I tell people about my personal SAVIOR, JESUS CHRIST.

I feel so good inside. It's a high and I want to feel like this for the rest of my life. I'm not afraid to die anymore, either.

I leave you with this: If you don't have in your life what I have, you'd better do whatever you have to do to get it!! You will never regret it for the rest of your life.

> Love you and God bless you,
> Robert Knowles

The best part of this story, though, is the afterword. It is often the case that after the initial

Delight thyself also in the LORD; and he shall give thee the desires of thine heart (Ps. 37:4).

enthusiasm and glow has subsided for the new Christian, he or she seems to permanently lose some of that fire. Happily, Robert's new relationship with Christ — begun in those countless parental prayers over many years — is anything but dampened. If anything, Robert needs someone to walk behind him with a fire extinguisher, because...well, let Carol tell it: "He is telling everywhere he goes, 'I have given my life to the Lord!'" Carol adds this bit of joy: "You know, I cannot remember him singing when he was a child, but he sings all the time now. He is still as on fire as the day God touched him, and we are praising God for it."

Surely you've guessed by now the "secret" of the Knowleses' success in reaching a wayward son: "We prayed a long time for him to know the Lord. It might be an inspiration to others to never give up praying for their loved ones."

Look long and see the power of Christ to change a life. A man who was too tough to show emotion, too independent to need anyone or anything . . . now sings his way through each day. The old rebel Judd Knowles sees it and he identifies. He'd rather his son's conversion had come sooner, but he'll gratefully take later.

WHEN I WAS A BOY OF 1 4,
MY FATHER WAS SO IGNORANT
I COULD HARDLY STAND TO HAVE
THE OLD MAN AROUND. BUT
WHEN I GOT TO BE 2 1, I WAS
ASTONISHED AT HOW MUCH
THE OLD MAN HAD LEARNED
IN SEVEN YEARS!

MARK TWAIN (1 8 3 5 – 1 9 1 O)

Delight thyself also in the LORD; and he shall give thee the desires of thine heart (Ps. 37:4).

DAD

CHAPTER FIVE

A NEW VOICE

JESUS SAID, "SUFFER THE LITTLE CHILDREN TO COME UNTO ME, AND FORBID THEM NOT: FOR SUCH IS THE KINGDOM OF GOD." HE CONTINUED, "VERILY I SAY UNTO YOU, WHOSOEVER SHALL NOT RECEIVE THE KINGDOM OF GOD AS A LITTLE CHILD, HE SHALL NOT ENTER THEREIN." OF COURSE, HE WAS NOT SPEAKING LITERALLY — GOD'S GIFT OF GRACE IS AVAILABLE AT ANY AGE, BUT IT'S SINCERE HUMILITY AND CHILDLIKE FAITH THAT HE WILL NOT TURN AWAY.

Pat Summerall, one of the most well-known voices and faces associated with the National Football League over the last 40 years, has now become a faithful voice for his new faith in Jesus Christ — thanks to a remarkable transformation in his life.

The popular Sunday afternoon voice of FOX-TV NFL football has become a regular speaker about his new life and journey from the depths of alcohol-laced despair to a new life in Christ.

"Pat's been truly part of a transformation experience in his own life and the transformation is still occurring," says his Dallas-area pastor Claude Thomas. "It's part of what it says in Romans 8 that God is changing us, and Romans 12:1–2 that we all have a transformation experience."

Asked to explain the change in his own life over the last couple of years, Summerall, 70, is for once at a momentary loss for words.

"I don't know what to say. It's just what happened

For he saith, I have heard thee in a time accepted, and in the day of salvation have I succoured thee: behold, now is the accepted time; behold, now is the day of salvation (2 Cor. 6:2).

DAD

to me; this is my story. I don't really know what to call it, but our home is named 'Amazing Grace,' so I thought about, 'The Hour I First Believed' or 'Grace Shall Lead Me Home.' "

Summerall was baptized at the age of 69 at First Baptist Church in Euless, Texas, outside of Dallas. He is now seeking to live a consistent Christian life, with help from a regular Bible study, church fellowship when he is in town, and regular growth — while balancing a busy schedule in a fast-paced and highly competitive work environment.

From the outside, Summerall's life has always appeared to be an All-America story. A prep football star in Florida, he attended the University of Arkansas and became a star kicker for the Razorbacks. He went on to play in the NFL and started for the New York Giants, playing under assistant coach Tom Landry.

After his football career was over, Summerall went into broadcasting. In addition to his football broadcasting, he also became the signature voice of the Masters Golf Tournament and the U.S. Open Tennis Tournament while at CBS. He then moved to FOX to broadcast football. He is entering his 22nd season overall with partner John Madden.

Summerall freely admits he became an alcoholic while broadcasting on TV and was ultimately living from drink to drink as his body broke down.

He had been an only child, and his parents divorced before he was born. He says that left him with a sense of emptiness and aloneness.

He first realized the need for a change during the 1994 Masters Tournament in Augusta, Georgia, the night after making his annual stop at the liquor store to fill up his house for a week-long party.

"I had been getting sick a lot, throwing up blood — and I got sick again at 4 a.m. I looked in the mirror, and the lights started to glow brighter until I saw what a terrible sight I was. I said to myself, *This is not the way I want to live.*

For he saith, I have heard thee in a time accepted, and in the day of salvation have I succoured thee: behold, now is the accepted time; behold, now is the day of salvation (2 Cor. 6:2).

A week later, Summerall was lured into a secret meeting, which included 13 of his closest friends and family members. Also, there were some big-name sports and TV figures — all pleading with him to get some help for his drinking problem. His daughter was there as well, and she told him that she had lately been ashamed to have his same last name.

Summerall spent 33 days in the Betty Ford Center in Palm Springs, California, which helped cure his alcohol problems. It didn't, however, fully address his spiritual vacuum.

After one of his first speeches about his medical recovery, Summerall bumped into his old coach, Landry, who helped explain about the spiritual need he still had in his life.

Summerall was also directed to long-time Dallas Cowboys chaplain John Weber, and that is when he began attending Pastor Thomas' church near his home.

"Pat is a great story of God's wonderful redeeming grace," Weber says. "Pat is very real, very honest, very candid about his life. He has a realistic approach about where he has been, but he doesn't glory in the past."

One night while talking with Thomas in his house, Summerall shared his story of transformation and asked about the requirements of joining the church. The pastor talked with him about baptism and church membership and what Summerall could be doing to affirm his new walk in Christ.

"He was already in the process of his spiritual journey, and I'm just so glad I was able to come alongside of him and help and encourage him in this time. I told Pat God has given him a unique platform.

"God used him in a mighty way with his long-time friend Mickey Mantle in speaking with Mantle about the Lord in his final days," Thomas says.

Summerall says he had been around rough and tough football players all of his life, but when he was baptized before a large congregation at FBC-Euless, he felt totally helpless. "I went down in the water, and

For he saith, I have heard thee in a time accepted, and in the day of salvation have I succoured thee: behold, now is the accepted time; behold, now is the day of salvation (2 Cor. 6:2).

when I came up, it was like a 40-pound weight had been lifted from me," Summerall says. "I have a happier life, a healthy life, and a more positive feeling about life than ever before."

Weber says others are quick to see a difference in Summerall, who once was the life of every party with a drink in his hand. Now he gets his power and life from another source.

"I'm so happy for Pat Summerall," Weber says. "He is one of the most positive, delightful persons to be around. He is one of the most complete and successful people in his business, and now is one of the nicest."

Thomas said he has watched Summerall's work on TV for a good portion of his adult life and is thrilled that his professional excellence is now matched by his personal peace.

"What Pat presents to me is the entire spectrum of pro football," Thomas says. "He is as current as today, but has the voice and experience of yesterday."

Summerall runs a production facility in Dallas, where he does a lot of off-season work in commercials and specials. He also works with Dallas-based motivator Zig Ziglar on occasion.

"I remember Zig once saying that with Jesus, you are never an only child, and that meant a lot to me because I had always been an only child and had always been lonely, but I don't have to feel lonely any more."

Every summer before the NFL season starts and every week before their feature game, Summerall and Madden take a tour of the NFL teams or visit with the teams they are going to be broadcasting that week.

Summerall said one week before broadcasting a Dallas-Green Bay game, they met with a coach who told them a true story about Packers Hall-of-Fame defensive end Reggie White and Dallas guard Larry Allen, then a rookie. Summerall says the story makes a vital point about his new faith.

For he saith, I have heard thee in a time accepted, and in the day of salvation have I succoured thee: behold, now is the accepted time; behold, now is the day of salvation (2 Cor. 6:2).

DAD

"Reggie White lined up against Larry Allen and on one snap, gave him a good club move and almost decapitated Troy Aikman," Summerall says. On the next series of downs, Allen gave White a few choice words, but at the snap White slipped past him and buried Aikman once again.

"As he headed back to his huddle, White looked down on the fallen Allen and said, 'Rookie, Jesus is coming, and you're not ready.'"

"Now at last, I know I'm ready, and I hope you are as well."

Words to remember from football's most recognizable voice.[2]

— Art Stricklin

Curt Schilling, co-winner of the 2001 World Series MVP award (his team, the Arizona Diamondbacks, came from behind to beat the New York Yankees in the seventh game of the series), says that his dad is still his best friend. Cliff Schilling died of cancer in 1988, and starting in that year, Curt has put his dad's name on the free-ticket list of every game in which he has started. By the time of the 2001 World Series, a seat of honor had been reserved for Cliff Schilling in over 290 games.

For he saith, I have heard thee in a time accepted, and in the day of salvation have I succoured thee: behold, now is the accepted time; behold, now is the day of salvation (2 Cor. 6:2).

Only a Dad

by Edgar Guest

Only a dad with a tired face,
Coming home from the daily race,
Bringing little of gold or fame
To show how well he has played the game;
But glad in his heart that his own rejoice
To see him come and to hear his voice.

Only a dad with a brood of four,
One of ten million men or more
Plodding along in the daily strife,
Bearing the whips and scorn of life,
With never a whimper of pain or hate,
For the sake of those who at home await.

Only a dad, neither rich nor proud,
Merely one of the surging crowd,
Toiling, striving from day to day,
Facing whatever may come his way,
Silent whenever the harsh condemn,
And bearing it all for the love of them.

Only a dad but he gives his all,
To smooth the way for his children small,
Doing with courage stern and grim
The deeds that his father did for him.
This is the line that for him I pen:
Only a dad, but the best of men.

Honor thy father and mother; which is the first commandment with promise (Eph. 6:2).

~ CHAPTER SIX ~

WOUNDED SOLDIER

WARTIME IS A TIME OF HIGH ANXIETY
AND INTENSITY AS MEN AND WOMEN
GO TO PLACES THEY HAVE NEVER BEEN,
SOMETIMES NEVER EVEN HEARD OF, TO
FACE AN ENEMY THEY DON'T KNOW.
MEANS OF COMMUNICATION AT THESE
TIMES ARE PRECIOUS AND FEW.

John Steer was one of over eight million U.S.
soldiers to fight in the Vietnam War. He was only 19
when he fought on Hill 875 in November of 1967,
probably the most intense fighting of the war. Before
they began advancing up the hill, he and his comrades
in "A" Company had been told that none of them
would be coming back. Hill 875 was a mountainous

area covered with thick jungle. The enemy had built an elaborate system of tunnels all through the mountain where they waited in hiding, popping up very quickly to kill the Americans coming up the mountain.

In the merciless bloodbath that followed, John Steer miraculously survived, but lost most of his right leg and right arm. Waiting for help to arrive, he hid himself under two corpses for protection, all the time in extreme pain. After losing much blood, he passed out, not knowing how long he laid there before any help arrived. He was taken away from a clearing in the jungle by a helicopter, constantly under fire, and then taken to a hospital in Japan. The doctors saved his leg, but could not save his arm.

The second day in the hospital, he decided to write his folks a letter. Although he was very confused, bitter, and angry, he tried not to let it show as he took the pen in his left hand. Since it was the first thing he had ever written using his left hand, it took some doing,

And he shall judge among the nations . . . and they shall beat their swords into plowshares, and their spears into pruninghooks: nation shall not lift up sword against nation, neither shall they learn war any more (Isa. 2:4).

DAD

but he made it. He was determined to show everyone he was tough and could function with one hand.

Dear Mom and Dad,

How are you I am doing all rite my writing is prety bad because I half to write with my left hand. They change my bandages and wash my wounds 3 times a day it's a pretty painful process The food here is great. And so is the service. They will probably start operating on my leg in about 3 or 4 days. And then my sholder. They have my right arm in traction They are trying to strech the skin over the bone. Doen't worry about me I will be good as new, it will just take a little time.

Take care   God bless
Love, John

P.S. Tell everybody I'm thinking about them.

Dear mom and dad, how are you I am doing allrite my writeing is pretty bad because I help to eat with my left hand. They change my bindages and wash my wounds 3 times a day it's a pretty painfull process. The food here is great. and so is the service. they will probably start opperating on my leg in about 3 or 4 days. and than my sholder. They have my right arm in traction. They are trying to strech the skin over the bone. Doen't worry about me I will be good as new, it will just take a little time.

Take care God bless

Love John

P.S. tell everybody I'm thinking about them.

And he shall judge among the nations . . . and they shall beat their swords into plowshares, and their spears into pruninghooks: nation shall not lift up sword against nation, neither shall they learn war any more (Isa. 2:4).

Now, stop and think about all the wars there have been. The United States alone has been involved in ten wars beginning with the Revolution. For each of those wars there are thousands — even millions — of soldiers. For each of those soldiers there is a family back home waiting, hoping, expecting to hear good news. Throughout all of these conflicts, the letter has been the chief means of communication. Millions have been sent. Can you imagine the anxiety and emotion felt as the recipient holds the envelope in hand, just before it is opened — the things going through his or her mind? One letter can mean exuberant joy or emotional pain. Or what about the *lack* of a letter?

During the Civil War, the story is told of President Lincoln summoning to the White House a surgeon in the Army of the Cumberland from the state of Ohio. Being asked personally to visit the president was such a high honor. The major beamed with pride as he assumed that he was to be commended for some exceptional work.

Upon entering the room where the president was, the two struck up a conversation mainly about the war and the particular action the surgeon had seen. Suddenly, the president changed the subject and asked the major bluntly about his widowed mother.

"She is doing fine," he responded.

"How do you know?" asked Lincoln. "You haven't written her."

The major cast his eyes to the floor and gripped his hat tightly.

"But she has written me," Lincoln continued. "She thinks that you are dead and she has asked that a special effort be made to return your body." The commander in chief said no more, but rose and placed a pen in the young doctor's hand. "Write to your mother and let her know that you are alive and well."

And he shall judge among the nations . . . and they shall beat their swords into plowshares, and their spears into pruninghooks: nation shall not lift up sword against nation, neither shall they learn war any more (Isa. 2:4).

DAD

CHAPTER SEVEN

LETTERS FROM CAMP

SUMMER CAMP IS A MODERN TRADITION
WHERE CHILDREN CAN GO AWAY FROM
HOME FOR A WEEK OR TWO, AND, UNDER
THE TUTELAGE OF A COUNSELOR WHO IS
USUALLY NOT MUCH OLDER THAN HIS OR
HER WARDS, THE CHILDREN CAN LEARN
ABOUT RESPONSIBILITY, INTEGRITY,
SWIMMING, CRAFTS, HOW TO RECOGNIZE
POISON IVY, AND, OF COURSE, EACH
RECEIVES A BONUS CRASH COURSE IN
LETTER WRITING.

Taylor Schall was not really the outgoing,
garrulous, buddy-buddy type of boy. He was more the
quiet and withdrawn type, content to be alone,

shooting baskets with a basketball in the driveway or reading a book. There was nothing that he liked better than home, with the entire family gathered around. For Taylor, that brought great feelings of warmth, love, and security.

To help the eight-year-old learn to function in a nurturing environment away from the family, his parents, Steve and Debbie, had a great idea. They made the decision to send Taylor off to a Christian camp for a couple of weeks in the summer. Surely in that sheltered environment, he would learn to mix and mingle with others his age and "come out of his shell." In the weeks leading up to the day that they would take him to camp, Steve and Debbie spent a lot of time assuring him of their love and reminding him about all the fun and adventure that he would have there at camp.

The big day finally arrived, and his parents drove into a neighboring state to the camp and dropped him off. Others who had arrived earlier already seemed to

I have learned, in whatsoever state I am, therewith to be content (Phil. 4:11).

DAD

be getting to know each other and it appeared to be an amiable, fun atmosphere there at camp. After waiting around long enough to make sure everything was okay, Steve and Debbie headed away from the camp and out of the country for a short-term mission trip.

Five days later, the mission trip was over, and Steve and Debbie had just arrived back home, and were going through the past week's mail. They sat down at the table and began looking earnestly through the stack of mail for envelopes with the camp's logo. They found five requisite letters from Taylor at camp. Sorting them by postmark date, Steve opened up the first letter and he and Debbie both began to read to themselves.

Steve and Debbie looked at each other, but

Dear Mom & Dad, I miss you a Lot! PICK ME UP! PLease, TAYLOR S.

didn't say anything. They reasoned that it was written by Taylor on his first day and it would just take him a little longer to get used to things at camp. They opened up the second letter.

Now Steve and Debbie were beginning to wonder if they had done the right thing. Maybe Taylor just wasn't quite ready to grow in this area of relating to others besides his family. They

Dear Mom + Dad
If I do not call
Tomorrow come pick me
up! Kamp is not going good
at all. I miss you a
LOT! please
come pick me
up!
Please!
Taylor

Dear Mom + Dad,
I'm serious! please pick me
up. If I do not call tomorrow!
PLEASE!
I miss you! I hate 2
weeks! I Love you!
PLEASE,
TAYLOR SCHALL

quickly opened up the third letter; they read.

Steve pushed his chair back and got up from the table. He was ready to instantly start on the trip to pick up Taylor from the camp. Just as he was reaching for

I have learned, in whatsoever state I am, therewith to be content (Phil. 4:11).

the telephone to call the camp, Debbie suggested reading the last couple of letters. Somewhat reluctantly, he picked up the fourth letter. At that letter, he laughed out loud. The fifth one was similar, as were all the rest of them that arrived the next week until Steve and Debbie arrived at closing ceremonies to pick up this boy who had turned the corner after the third day (as Scott, the counselor, put it) and had the time of his life (as Taylor put it).

> Dear Mom & Dad,
> Kamps Great!
> I Love you a lot!
> Geuss what. I was the only person to get a gold K in high jump! We had our looney tune party! It was a blast!
> SCOTT IS COOL!
> Love,
> TAYLOR

Looking back, that camp experience was a major turning point for Taylor. Like his father, he still prefers home to just about any other place on the planet; but he has also grown by leaps and bounds in his ability to relate to others and gain joy from building relationships outside of the family.

My father used to play with my brother and me in the yard. Mother would come out and say, "You're tearing up the grass." "We're not raising grass," Dad would reply. "We're raising boys."
— Harmon Killebrew

I have learned, in whatsoever state I am, therewith to be content (Phil. 4:11).

DAD

CHAPTER EIGHT

THE GOOD PROVIDER

"WHAT DOES A DAD DO?" SEEMS TO BE A
QUESTION TOO MANY OF OUR CHILDREN
ASK BECAUSE THEY'VE NEVER SEEN A DAD
IN ACTION. THE IMPORTANCE OF A DAD
AROUND THE HOUSE CANNOT BE
UNDERESTIMATED — TO SET AN
EXAMPLE, TO GUIDE, TO TEACH, TO LOVE
— TO DO THOSE THINGS THAT A MOM
JUST CAN'T ALWAYS DO.

If there was one thing I wasn't afraid of, it was
work. In fact, working harder was sometimes the only
thing that made me feel good. So when Tami and I
were expecting our third child back in 1991, it made
perfect sense that I would simply have to put in more

hours as a computer programmer. How else was I going to support the house full of kids that Tami and I yearned to have?

The company I worked for — Millstone Coffee — was giving portable computers to their traveling personnel to keep track of sales and inventory on the road. One of my jobs was designing applications for the programs those computers use. One day a rep for a computer manufacturer approached me and asked if I could do a similar job for his company on the side. The project consumed all my free time but put $5,000 in our bank account — a small fortune, and enough to ease our fears about the new addition to our household. *Not bad*, I thought.

It wasn't long after Eve was born that I came up with the idea of going into business for myself. I brought up the idea one night at dinner. "I can keep my job at Millstone and do other work on the side," I told Tami. "It'll mean extra hours on nights and weekends. But I know I can handle it."

But if any provide not for his own, and specially for those of his own house, he hath denied the faith, and is worse than an infidel (1 Tim. 5:8).

Tami looked down at her plate. "Jim, the money will be great. You don't need to tell me how useful it would be. But don't forget what happened to your dad."

Dad. How could I ever forget? Dad had wanted the best for my brother and my sisters and me. He'd paid his own way through college, working two jobs. By the time we kids came along, he had a good solid position as a government biologist. But he also had a secret. At school, he'd picked up the habit of relying on amphetamines to keep his energy up, using them to get through the grueling schedule of responsibilities he had set for himself.

Dad's secret weapon turned into an ugly, humiliating drug habit. His reputation nose-dived. He unraveled inside as well. Too young to understand what was really happening to him, I still knew *something* was terribly wrong. It killed me to see the person I most loved and admired in the world come home with that jumpy, frightened look on his face night after night. "Why is Dad so tired?" I'd ask my mom. "Is it my fault?"

"He'll be all right, dear," Mom would say. "He just wants the best for us, so he needs to work extra hard." Finally, Dad had a breakdown and was hospitalized. He was never the same after that. The man for whom hard work was its own reward couldn't hold down a job anymore. He and Mom divorced. Dad drifted in and out of institutions and shelters. In 1987, the same year Tami and I were married, he took his own life.

"Don't worry," I told Tami that night at dinner. "I know what I'm doing. I'm tired of cramped apartments and broken-down cars. There's so much I want to give you guys, but I can't do it without going the extra mile."

I worked weekends and late into the night. It paid off. One Saturday morning I brought Tami into our kitchen and sat her down in front of two neat stacks of paper. "These are purchase orders from companies

But if any provide not for his own, and specially for those of his own house, he hath denied the faith, and is worse than an infidel (1 Tim. 5:8).

for the software I've created," I told her. "This stack here is going to pay for a car big enough for all the kids to fit in. And this stack next to it is going to give us a down payment for a house of our own."

Tami was speechless, and I felt a charge run through me I couldn't find words for, a simply incredible feeling. I was providing for my family, giving them all the things they wanted and deserved. I felt strong, accomplished, needed.

In 1993, Tami gave birth to Grace, our fourth child, and I made another leap of faith, quitting my job with Millstone and devoting myself full-time to my company — now christened Versatile Systems. As my family grew, so did my ambitions. I hired a staff of half a dozen people and kept my eye on them every minute to make sure they did things the right way, my way. Most evenings I'd get home too late to see any of the kids at all.

"Daddy, why weren't you at the Christmas pageant last night?" Esther asked me one day.

"I wanted to be there, honey — I really did. But I had to work late. I tell you what, why don't I put a little something extra in your allowance this week to make up for it?" I caught a look from Tami. It wasn't exactly a happy one.

So it went. I'd come home zonked from another 15-hour day, only to be greeted with that look of hers. One night my cell phone went off while we were reading to the kids. I hesitated, then answered it. Tami snatched the book from my hand and continued herself.

All right, so I worked hard. Was that some kind of sin, though? Didn't the Bible command us to labor honestly? After all, I did it all for my family. Who else would provide for them if I didn't? Did they want me to end up like my dad? Why on earth couldn't Tami see that?

Then came February 1996, and Jael's sixth birthday. It was going to be her first "grown-up" party, and she was talking about it for weeks ahead of time.

But if any provide not for his own, and specially for those of his own house, he hath denied the faith, and is worse than an infidel (1 Tim. 5:8).

Tami let me know that I absolutely had to be there for it. But I had important business in San Francisco that I couldn't miss. I found a flight that would leave right after the meeting and get me back to Seattle in time for the party.

The meeting went off without a hitch. I was about to close a major deal, and I was pretty psyched about it. Then I got to the airport. My plane was delayed. *I've got to get home.* I tried to book another flight. No dice. I'd never make it. I sat down in the gate area and dialed the office on my cell phone. "The meeting went fine," I told my partner Frank. "But now I'm stuck at the airport and missing Jael's birthday." An awful feeling came over me suddenly, a flash of failure and emptiness. But I stuffed it away and pulled out my laptop. *I'll do some work. That will make me feel better.*

I pulled into our driveway at a little after six. A big bunch of balloons on our dining table greeted me forlornly. I looked at the message attached. "Sorry I'm late. Love you — Dad." *Must have been Frank's idea, I* thought. Tami came in from the backyard, a tired but smiling Jael right behind her. "Daddy!" Jael squealed.

"Happy birthday, honey," I said, scooping her up and giving her a big hug and a kiss. "At least those balloons made it on time," I offered weakly to Tami.

Jael led me out back to show me the presents her friends had given her. When we came back into the dining room a few minutes later, Tami was looking at the card attached to the balloons.

"You know, Jim, it's funny about this card — it really doesn't sound like you."

"Well, actually . . . I didn't send them. It must have been Frank's idea. He knew I was going to be late."

You could almost hear the snapping sound of that last straw breaking the camel's back. I braced for the torrent I knew was coming, the lecture I would get about neglecting my family and being an absentee father. But they didn't know what it was like to have an absent father the way mine was absent. He couldn't hold a job. He couldn't even hold onto his family's love.

But if any provide not for his own, and specially for those of his own house, he hath denied the faith, and is worse than an infidel (1 Tim. 5:8).

But no torrent came. "Jim," Tami said simply, holding up the card. "Don't you see what's happening to you?"

I looked at the writing on that card — those words to a person as dear to me as my own life, written by someone who didn't even know her — and I *did* see. I'd been knocking myself out to compensate for my father's tragic failure, to earn my family's love. But that love was the one thing that I didn't ever need to earn. It was right there waiting for me. All I had to do was *be there* to receive it.

Tami and I joined a family-counseling group at church, where I was reminded that the Bible also urges us to honor our families. Old habits are hard to shake, and old fears even harder. My father's failure to provide for his family had haunted me to the point where I was destroying myself as surely as he had.

One morning at work I called everyone into the conference room. "From now on," I said, "things are going to be a little different around here. My new hours will be Monday through Thursday, from nine to five — six at the latest. I won't be taking any calls on my days off, either. I've spent a lot of time in the past looking over your shoulders, but now I'm going to let you do your jobs yourselves." I could tell they were having a hard time holding back the cheers.

I think Tami and the kids wanted to cheer, too. All my life I'd wanted to be a good provider. Now, at last, I was.[3]

EACH DAY OF OUR LIVES WE
MAKE DEPOSITS IN THE MEMORY
BANKS OF OUR CHILDREN.
— CHARLES R. SWINDOLL, *THE STRONG FAMILY*

But if any provide not for his own, and specially for those of his own house, he hath denied the faith, and is worse than an infidel (1 Tim. 5:8).

DAD

CHAPTER NINE

WAKE-UP CALL

"... A DATE WHICH WILL LIVE IN INFAMY."
THESE WORDS WERE SPOKEN BY PRESIDENT
FRANKLIN ROOSEVELT DESCRIBING
DECEMBER 7, 1941, BUT THEY MIGHT
ALSO BE APPLIED TO SEPTEMBER 11,
2001 — SIXTY YEARS LATER. SEASONS
COME AND GO, TECHNOLOGY CHANGES
THINGS, BUT WE FIND THAT PEOPLE ARE
THE SAME. ANOTHER QUOTE FROM
ROOSEVELT IS ALSO STILL APPLICABLE
TODAY — "THE ONLY THING WE HAVE TO
FEAR IS FEAR ITSELF."

For all the staggering pain associated with the
terrorist attacks in America on September 11, 2001,

there was also — if we can admit it — much healing. An event of that magnitude cannot leave people the way they were. No one emerged unchanged. From New York to San Diego, it was as if a divine wind blew over damaged relationships. Gaping at the devastation in New York, Washington, and Pennsylvania, couples decided to heal their marriages. Siblings reconciled. Friends reached for address books to reconnect with one another.

Of course, there are stories that are forged in our collective memories: Todd Beamer leading a group of passengers on Flight 93, which crashed in a lonely Pennsylvania field . . . and not into the White House. Hollywood execs flying from Boston to L.A. who never made it. Cell phone conversations between trapped flyers and stricken loved ones back home. All these vignettes are wrapped around hearts the world over.

Then there were the stories known only to a few. Thousands of them. Those reconciliations that

For this my son was dead, and is alive again; he was lost, and is found. And they began to be merry (Luke 15:24).

were so sudden, so . . . unanticipated, we can't help but be captured by them. Here is one such story.

Billy had lived for years in Las Vegas, waiting tables, enjoying friends, living the single life. He liked living life his way. After all, this was "The Town Sinatra Built." Why not take a cue from Frank? Trouble was, all this self-centeredness left little time for family back home. Truthfully, it left no time. It had been years since Billy had seen his father, or even talked to him. Communicating wasn't on their agenda.

His father, Bill, was the classic tough guy. Ex-Marine, self-employed. No one told Bill what to do. Nobody wanted to; the reaction wasn't worth it. Gruff, he carried himself like a guy who'd rather hit someone than have a pleasant conversation. And emotion? Forget about it! This Chicago native was about as warm as Dick Butkus at Soldier Field in January. Bill didn't approve of Billy's lifestyle. Billy didn't approve of Bill not approving of his lifestyle. Bill didn't approve of Billy not approving . . . well, you get the point.

You see what kind of odds there were that this father and son would get together and reconcile. For Billy, it was easier to wait tables in a desert paradise and hang out with friends. At the same time, Bill was more than content to prop his feet up at the end of the day and sit on the deck of his lakefront home.

Then terrorists from half-a-world away invaded their lives. Invaded lives all over America.

Sitting on the edge of his bed on the morning of September 11, Billy tried to focus. It had been a late night at work. The patrons had loved Billy; his infectious personality brought more people into the restaurant. That made for long hours; Billy just couldn't get enough of the warmth he got from strangers.

Today he was in a fog. The television was still on from the time he arrived home early in the morning. Something was different, though. Something was wrong. There was no mindless banter between morning show hosts.

For this my son was dead, and is alive again; he was lost, and is found. And they began to be merry (Luke 15:24).

DAD

"Something has happened at the World Trade Center," the unsteady voice said. "We — we think that a plane has crashed into one of the towers."

Billy blinked and sat straight up. He rubbed his eyes, joining countless citizens across the country. Nothing got done that day at Billy's modest home. He tried to absorb the information overload, and he grew more panicked. The extent of the attacks wouldn't be known for several more hours. Billy was alone.

Suddenly, he picked up the phone and dialed a number he didn't know from memory. Deet, deet-deet-deet; deet, deet, deet, deet, deet, deet, deet.

It's ringing, he thought. *Pick up!*

"Hello?"

"Dad?"

"Billy?"

"I guess you've seen the news."

"Yeah, I've got it on, now. Bad deal."

"Dad?"

"Yeah?"

"You know I don't write letters. I don't even call."

"Yeah."

"Dad, consider this a letter. I've got to see you."

"Maybe we can get out there this summer...."

"No, you don't understand; I have to see you now. I love you, Dad."

The rest of the conversation was like so many others that day. A blur. Two days later, standing in his kitchen, stirring sugar into coffee, Bill heard a noise at the door. The face in the glass wasn't threatening. Threatened was more like it.

"Billy? What are you doing here?" Billy didn't wait to answer. He almost shot through the door. He hugged his father for the first time in a long, long time. Heck, maybe for the first time since the Bears won the Super Bowl. Bill didn't back up. A change had been taking place in his heart, too. Some months back, his wife, Sue, found some Christian friends and she found the Lord. Bill followed and that miracle

For this my son was dead, and is alive again; he was lost, and is found. And they began to be merry (Luke 15:24).

that God does so well lighted on another family.

Billy said later that the events of September 11 woke him up to the fact that he might never see his family again.

The weekend Billy spent with Bill and Sue probably won't be as well known as the heroic efforts of Todd Beamer, but this father and son found redemption all the same. Two men who didn't like each other very much are close again. They talk. They share. The bond is strong. It happened in a "letter" over the phone.

A LETTER FROM COLLEGE

Dear Dad,

I ju$t wanted to drop a line to you. How i$ Mom? How i$ $andy? I remember that you told me if I ever needed $omething, to ju$t a$k. Well, I gue$$ I'm doing $well. Why don't you write back $ometime, and if you wi$h to $end $omething el$e, ju$t $end it along!

Thank$,
Reggie

AND THE REPLY

Dear Son,

NOthing ever happens around here. NObody comes to visit. NObody calls. I've got a NOtion to take a vacation soon. We may go see your Uncle NOlan in KNOxville, or Aunt NOrene in FresNO. Who kNOws? Drop us aNOther NOte when you can, son.

With love,
Dad

For this my son was dead, and is alive again; he was lost, and is found. And they began to be merry (Luke 15:24).

DAD

~ CHAPTER TEN ~

DADDY'S LETTERS

JUDITH GILLIS

HAVE YOU EVER WONDERED ABOUT HOW YOU WILL BE REMEMBERED AFTER YOU ARE GONE? WILL THE MEMORIES OF YOU BE SWEET OR BITTER? HOPEFULLY, YOU WILL HAVE LEFT A GODLY HERITAGE THAT WILL CARRY ON FOR GENERATIONS AFTER YOU. JESUS SAID, "YE ARE THE SALT OF THE EARTH." OUR SALT SHOULD CONTINUE TO ADD SOME SPICE AND FLAVOR TO THE LIVES OF OTHERS LONG AFTER THE SHAKER IS GONE.

Daddy never wrote me a letter in his life that I can recall. Well, not with paper and ink like you'd think of a real letter. Except for that one, six months before he died. Daddy belonged to a generation of men who didn't think about writing letters. Writing letters was a woman's task. His work was to write life and beauty and incredible memories on my heart.

Daddy was a long, lean Texan with piercing green eyes. He could look right through me at 20 yards, or so it seemed to me, growing up. It used to fascinate me how the smoke from his cigarette curled up into his nose. How he'd squint one eye and softly whistle a tuneless melody as he sorted mica and quartz and geodes in battered cardboard boxes out in our shabby garage. I watched as his rough hands caressed the stones, the way I wished he'd caress my childish face.

The closest he ever got to tenderness was to call me Sugarbaby when the going got rough. A sentimental notion like writing a letter to his daughter was as foreign to him as working a steady job or voting Republican.

Growing up, home life was pretty stormy. Every

Ye are the salt of the earth: but if the salt have lost his savour, wherewith shall it be salted? It is thenceforth good for nothing but to be cast out (Matt. 5:13).

few months my parents would have a terrific blowup, louder and longer than their weekly fights. The *casus belli* was usually because Daddy had quarreled with his boss and quit his job, or invested his meager paycheck in some mining scheme, or given our grocery money to a down-and-out acquaintance. Our dwindling budget meant rent money was scarce, and Daddy needed to find another job. We moved every few months so he could find a boss more to his liking.

Meanwhile, I got used to stuffing and unstuffing cardboard boxes full of my dolls and books and childish paraphernalia. This was just the way life went. Pack, unpack, start a new school, make a friend or two, then pack up again and head for a different house in a different town. Before each move, Daddy would take me on his lap and promise for the thousandth time that someday, we'd have a little farm, he'd work the land, and we'd never have to move again.

Gradually, I developed a benign indifference to our gypsy life. In Daddy's mind though, the next place down the road would be the home where Mama would magically become happy, his daughter would adore him, and he could rock away the hours on an old front porch. He was a man who nursed a terrible ache in the deepest part of his soul for a place that didn't exist.

All the while, Daddy's writings were like everything else in his enigmatic life — unconventional. He was a "heart writer." He'd take me camping and we'd sit around a campfire as he'd weave vivid stories about his hardscrabble childhood on a Texas farm. A life so bleak and foreign to me, I still remember nearly every word 40 years later. Daddy's kind of prose was strumming his guitar and singing lonesome songs, some of his own composing, about trains, Texas, and lost love. Sometimes he sang with tears in his eyes, empathizing with imaginary cowpokes and their myriad troubles.

The tumult of my parent's unhappy marriage, their many separations, finally ended when one night,

Ye are the salt of the earth: but if the salt have lost his savour, wherewith shall it be salted? It is thenceforth good for nothing but to be cast out (Matt. 5:13).

DAD

after another uproar with my mother, he slammed out the back door with his suitcase, for good. After a childhood full of breakups and broken promises, I thought he'd be back in a month or two, like always. Just before he stepped out into the night, he turned back and called to me, "Don't you worry, Sugarbaby, I'll write you from wherever I'm at." No letters ever came.

Never.

Not one.

My hopeful trips to the mailbox became fewer and fewer until I just didn't bother to hope anymore. He'd slammed the door once too often, I guess. Years passed. I grew up, married, had a family, lived life, and stopped missing Daddy. It would be two decades before I laid eyes on him again.

In the midst of raising babies, carpooling, and coming to grips with being a parent, I became a Christian. After some months, a memory or two of Daddy would come to mind now and then, like a gentle nudge. The Lord was working on my indifferent heart. I'd wonder where Daddy was, what he was doing, what he looked like now. After a few minutes, I'd brush the thoughts aside. What would he care? It seemed Daddy had forgotten about me long ago. If he cared, he'd at least write and let me know he was alive. He'd ask about me, wouldn't he? He'd want to know if he had grandchildren.

In spite of my doubts, a metamorphosis was occurring. One day I found myself recalling a camping trip with Daddy when I was a girl. A curious warmth stole over me at the memory. Then the idea came. What would happen if I tried to contact him? An old acquaintance had his address. What if I wrote him and invited him back into my life? Would he step through the open door?

After a few days of praying and thinking about writing Daddy, on a rainy November day, I poured out my heart to him in a letter.

Ye are the salt of the earth: but if the salt have lost his savour, wherewith shall it be salted? It is thenceforth good for nothing but to be cast out (Matt. 5:13).

DAD

Daddy, I miss you after all these years and
think about you a lot. When your grandsons
look up at me, I see your hazel eyes. They have
your quick, light laugh, Daddy. The songs you
taught me, I'm teaching them. Jimmy is a born
poet; Joey is the troubadour. Maybe you could
write me sometime. Maybe you could come for
a visit. I guess that's all I wanted to say for now.

Love,
Your Sugarbaby

P.S. I've given my life to the Lord and I pray for
you.

Days passed, then weeks. No answer. One warm
morning in early spring, I walked out to the mailbox.
There it was! An envelope addressed to me in Daddy's
careful, deliberate script. With trembling fingers, I tore
it open. I could hardly breathe as I read.

Sugarbaby, it's been a long time. I didn't think you wanted to hear from me. I ain't much at writing letters (guess you figured that out, ha ha), but I just wanted to say, yes, I'd like to come and see you sometime, and your boys, too. How old are they? Did you tell them about me? Here is my phone number. Call me if you want to. I hope you do.

Love,
Daddy

P.S. Can you sill make cornbread like I showed you?

Yes. He'd said yes! He wanted to connect again. This was more than stories over a campfire, or songs. This one letter he'd managed to write mattered more than anything in the world.

A few days passed while I prayed for courage to call him. On a quiet Sunday afternoon, while the

Ye are the salt of the earth: but if the salt have lost his savour, wherewith shall it be salted? It is thenceforth good for nothing but to be cast out (Matt. 5:13).

children were napping, I dialed his number in Oregon. One, two, three rings ... then Daddy answered. I swallowed the lump in my throat and plunged ahead, "Daddy, hi! It's me!" Years melted away in a moment, as I heard his quiet laugh.

"Sugarbaby, is this really you?" I was nine years old again, hanging on his every word.

A few phone calls passed between us, each one longer and lighter and sweeter than the last. By the end of that summer, we both felt strong enough for a real visit. The boys watched bug-eyed as Daddy parked his battered pickup on our lawn. They ran their fingers over his snakeskin boots in amazement, and howled with glee at the outrageous stories he told them. Daddy regaled us with some of his songs, and smiled as the boys sang him their childish tunes. After the boys were tucked in bed, Daddy and I talked far into the night. We spoke words full of grace for one another. He regretted all the lost years, and I lamented my indifference toward him. Healing had finally come.

Forgiveness passed from heart to heart.

He held my hand for a long moment at the truck when it was time to go. Was it all right if he called me every week? Promises of a Christmas visit. Maybe the boys could come up and see him when school was out. We hugged and he slowly drove out for the long trip home.

That winter was a brutal one, everywhere. Daddy phoned to say the snow was so deep around his trailer, he could hardly see out over the drifts. Cold he couldn't shake seeped into his lungs. He called the next week to tell me about his cough and to say he was writing a new song. In the spring, he'd take it to an old buddy who worked in a recording studio in Los Angeles.

A week passed, no call. I didn't think much about it; sometimes he'd miss a week, now and then. I purposed to call him in a few days and we'd swap snow stories. A few evenings later, I was drying dishes when the phone rang. Everything slowed to a surreal

Ye are the salt of the earth: but if the salt have lost his savour, wherewith shall it be salted? It is thenceforth good for nothing but to be cast out (Matt. 5:13).

DAD

tempo ... my cousin's voice ... "I'm so sorry ... came over to visit your Daddy ... high fever. ... I tried to get him to the doctor ... he died on the way to the hospital ... pneumonia they said."

The house is quieter now. The boys are married with children of their own. Sometimes I sit in my attic and finger yellowed pages of songs he composed, scribing feelings he could not share in any other way. Daddy's lyrics echo through his grandsons' poetry. Their songs are partly his, partly theirs. His laughter tumbles down the days into their banter and quick humor. I close my eyes and smile as I remember him around a hundred campfires, me drowsing in my sleeping bag under a sky full of shimmering stars. I smell the acrid wood smoke and feel a night breeze on my cheek. His voice comes back clear and steady in my mind, and I chuckle as I recall his yarns. These were the only letters he could write. His beautiful, beautiful letters. The only ones I'll ever need.

IT IS ADMIRABLE FOR A MAN TO
TAKE HIS SON FISHING,
BUT THERE IS A SPECIAL PLACE
IN HEAVEN FOR THE FATHER WHO
TAKES HIS DAUGHTER SHOPPING.
— JOHN SINOR

Ye are the salt of the earth: but if the salt have lost his savour, wherewith shall it be salted? It is thenceforth good for nothing but to be cast out (Matt. 5:13).

DAD

CHAPTER ELEVEN

THE RACE

BIOLOGICALLY SPEAKING, EVERYONE HAS A FATHER. BUT, IN REALITY, IT IS A RARE PRIVILEGE TO GROW UP UNDER THE CARE AND EXAMPLE OF ONE'S BIOLOGICAL FATHER. EVEN AT THAT, SOME CHILDREN ARE PUT ASIDE OR IGNORED BY THEIR OWN DAD, FOR BUSINESS REASONS, OR PLEASURE, OR SIMPLY BECAUSE OF SELFISHNESS. EVEN WHEN THEY DON'T MEAN TO FAIL, OUR DADS WILL SOMETIMES NOT COME THROUGH WHEN WE NEED THEM. HOWEVER, WE CAN ALWAYS BE ASSURED THAT OUR HEAVENLY FATHER WILL NEVER LEAVE US NOR FORSAKE US.

Matthew was ten years old and had been in Cub Scouts only a short time. He loved the den meetings and the friends he had made in the scouts. He had already finished some of the projects in the *Cub Scout Handbook,* even surprising himself with his achievements.

During one of his meetings, he was handed a sheet of instructions, a small block of wood, and four small tires. All of the scouts were told to go home from the meeting and seek their dads' help in building a model racing car for the Pinewood Derby. Matt began to dread the project immediately.

Before he had joined the scouts, his mother had reminded him, "Now, Matt, I want you to think about this before you join. You know you won't get much help out of your father. You'll be doing a lot of this on your own. Now, do you still want to join?"

He thought awhile, knowing that his father was a workaholic who rarely spent time with him. Instead of feeling sorry for himself, he had looked at his mother

Lo, children are an heritage of the LORD
(Ps. 127:3).

and replied, "Yeah, Mom. I know, but I still want to join. I know the Lord will help me."

Matt walked home from the meeting and thought about the project. His eyes scanned the instructions and specifications about the car. It didn't look too difficult, but Matt had never been good at arts and crafts. He didn't know much about woodworking, but he made up his mind he would give it a try. He *had* to try. His Sunday school teacher's words from the day before suddenly came back to him. "I can do all things through Christ which strengtheneth me." He thought about that. *All things. All things.* A determination welled up inside of him as he brushed back the tears and thought, *I can do this. I CAN DO THIS!* Then he prayed a silent prayer for help.

Not having a garage or workbench, Matt began working on his project in his bedroom. Every afternoon after school, he would work on his project. He followed the directions to the best of his ability, and the little block of wood began to look like a model racecar. It wasn't perfect, but with the encouragement of his mother, Matt felt pretty proud of his achievement. It *really did* look like a racecar. He felt it was the best project he had ever done, and his mom thought so, too. He named his car *Blue Lightning*.

The big night of the Pinewood Derby race finally came. Matt entered the school cafeteria smiling and holding his car in front of him like a proud craftsman. His smile quickly faded, however, when he saw the cars of the other boys. Neat, sleek, shiny, and slick. It was obvious that most of them had had help from their parents in the construction of their cars. Matt's car was lopsided, wobbly, and unattractive compared to theirs, and he quickly clutched it close to his chest, hoping no one would notice it. As he tried to disappear into the crowd, a boy said, "Matt, let me see your car." He giggled when he saw Matt's car. Others would giggle or snicker, or smile smugly as they showed him their cars.

To add to his humility, Matt was the only boy

Lo, children are an heritage of the LORD
(Ps. 127:3).

there without a man beside him. Even a couple of boys who lived with only their mom had a grandfather or an uncle there. Matt only had his mom.

The races began. The cars were not motorized in any way; they coasted down a ramp to the bottom and the first one to the bottom was determined the winner of each race. All of the cars didn't race at once. Only two were raced at a time with the winner going on to challenge others. Names had been drawn to match up the participants, and Matt would be in the final race of the first heat.

As the race prior to his race ended, and the crowd clapped and cheered for the winner, Matt's heart began to pound with excitement. His opponent's car looked fast — very fast. It looked like it could beat any car there. The owner of that car and his father exchanged glances as they took a look at Matt's car. Just before the race was to begin, Matt signaled the scoutmaster in charge. It took a moment to get the man's attention, but he finally looked at

Matt, who asked, "Can we pray before this race?" Matt's mom's stomach filled with butterflies. Matt was usually so shy that a request like this in a crowd like this was very unusual for him. She was very surprised and looked at the scoutmaster, who had a strange, blank look on his face.

The scoutmaster shrugged his shoulders and said, "That would be okay," and everyone bowed their heads in respect. Some even closed their eyes, although most were peeking at Matt, who clutched his car tightly in his hands and knelt on his knees in silent prayer. His face showed an earnestness as he wrinkled his brow and moved his lips. After what seemed to be a very long minute and a half, he stood up, smiled, and said, "Okay, I'm ready."

The boys placed their cars in the starting blocks, and waited for the signal. At the flag, the gates opened and the two cars went speeding down the ramp. Matt's eyes were full of anticipation and surprise as the two cars stayed neck-and-neck, closing in on the finish

Lo, children are an heritage of the LORD
(Ps. 127:3).

line. The crowd was yelling and cheering for one or the other and some were jumping up and down. The race was over in a matter of seconds, but it seemed much longer to Matt as he watched excitedly. The cheer rose to a crescendo as Matt's car crossed the finish line just slightly ahead of the other car.

Matt leaped into the air with a loud "Thank You!" and he jumped and jumped and tried to hug his mother as he jumped, and her purse fell off of her arm, and everyone was watching and yelling and cheering and clapping and others were hugging Matt or trying to pat him on the back.

The scoutmaster began to shush the crowd, loudly saying, "Okay, okay!" as he waved his arms up and down like he was trying to press the noise down. The roar finally diminished enough for the scoutmaster to ask Matt, "So you prayed to win, huh?"

You could have heard a pin drop as all eyes turned to Matt who stood there, grinning from ear to ear. He said, "Oh, no, sir. That wouldn't be fair to ask

God to help you beat someone else. I just asked Him to make it so I don't cry when I lose."

Matt's mom was the one who was crying.

As he lay in bed that night, Matt sent a mental thank-you note above:

Dear Heavenly Father,
    Thank you for helping me tonight and with the whole project. Also, Lord, would You please get my dad to go to church with me and Mom, so he will be saved and know You, too? Thank You. Amen.

Bear ye one another's burdens, and so fulfill the law of Christ (Ps. 127:3).

DAD

CHAPTER TWELVE

PROMISES KEPT

SHIRLEY MITCHELL

CHARLES SWINDOLL ONCE ADMONISHED HIS LISTENERS, "BE AUTHENTIC." ONE OF THE HARDEST THINGS ABOUT BEING A CHRISTIAN PARENT IS TO LIVE WHAT YOU TEACH. "DON'T DO AS I DO; DO AS I SAY" IS AN ALL-TOO-COMMON PHRASE. THE BIBLE TEACHES THAT WE ARE LIVING EPISTLES, AND, AS SUCH, WE NEED TO BECOME LIVING EXAMPLES OF THE WORD OF GOD AND THE LOVE OF CHRIST.

The slow drip of the IV nourished and medicated my father as he lay, seemingly lifeless, on the sterile white hospital bed. Like a crown of glory, his white hair blended into the white pillow.

Staring at the frail form on the bed, I couldn't believe that in his prime, my dad had weighed 200 pounds. I watched from a chair in the corner of the dimly lit room and remembered his younger, stronger body. My dad always had excellent posture. He walked with an aura of confidence until a stroke slowed his pace.

I wanted to talk to him, to tell him how much I loved him, but I couldn't. I sat there in that hospital room by a little table, and I noticed a pen and pad lying there. *That's it,* I thought. *I'll write Dad a letter.* As I took the pen in hand and began to write, however, I found it a little more difficult than what I thought it would be to write down how I really felt about this wonderful man who had raised me to adulthood, teaching me so much about life along the way.

Let us hold fast the profession of our faith without wavering (for he is faithful that promised) (Heb. 10:23).

DAD

Dear Dad,

I wish I could talk to you right now to tell you how much I love you. You are still asleep, so I'm not able to talk to you, but I'll write you a letter.

Your character, faith, and balance gave me a life centered in Christ. You taught by example. I learned that promises were made to be kept because you always kept your promises. For instance, the time you promised me a new piano....

The dim, bleak mood of the hospital room changed with a mental flashback of Dad sweeping me off the ground in his hard, strong arms and whirling me around him. It was a Saturday — a very special Saturday for this ten-year-old girl from Alabama. Dad put me down, and I began prancing around the wagon pulled by a tractor; in the wagon was what had just become my prized possession — my piano.

My parents were cotton farmers and had to make every penny count. We lived on a cotton farm in a square white house, with four equal rooms, built by my dad in the middle of the potato patch. We were poor and didn't have many possessions so you can imagine the thrill I felt over getting a piano, even if it was given to us by my grandparents who lived nearby.

The highlight of every week came each Saturday morning when I walked two miles to my cherished piano lesson. I had been practicing at my grandparents' house, but now I could stay home and practice. That I could own a piano and take lessons was a miracle that I thought could only be by divine providence, brought to life by parents who dreamed and planned to make it happen. This morning, moving my precious piano to our new home preceded even piano lessons in importance. I ran happily, giggling, as Dad began to cautiously drive the tractor toward our front door.

The cotton-farming region where we lived did not have many trees, but we did have a mighty oak

Let us hold fast the profession of our faith without wavering (for he is faithful that promised) (Heb. 10:23).

tree by our house. I always loved that tree — until that morning. As my dad slowly moved closer to his destination, he failed to see the root of that old oak tree sticking up a few inches above the ground. The tractor crossed over the root without a hitch, but the when the front right wagon wheel hit the root, it jarred the whole wagon enough to dislodge the massive old upright piano. I watched in disbelief as it first tipped, then fell, then bounced out onto the hard ground and rolled over and over, breaking into a thousand splinters.

The magnitude of my loss sank deep into my soul. I ran, screamed, and cried. My dad caught me, picked me up in his strong arms, and hugged me to him as I beat upon his broad shoulders with my small clenched fists. "You broke my piano!" I screamed into his ear. He held my trembling body firmly to his bosom until I stopped sobbing. His big, green eyes looked deeply into my bewildered, dark brown ones. His face looked sad, but he said, "Before, I die, I will buy you a new piano."

A decade went by and another. I married, moved away with my husband, and we were raising three children. The last thing I thought about was a piano.

One day the doorbell rang. A piano salesman introduced himself politely and said, "Your dad has paid for any piano you would like." He handed me a catalog filled with all kinds of pianos. Through my tears I selected my favorite.

Well, my mind went on from one memory to another in that hospital room, and I fell asleep, never finishing the letter.

Today, I find myself thinking of memories of my youth in Alabama. I love playing my piano. My children learned to play on it, and now my six grandchildren touch the ivory keys. My piano occupies a special place in my living room and in my heart. That special place in my heart is filled with sadness, because my dad now has a new home in heaven. The sadness is for me, because I miss him.

Let us hold fast the profession of our faith without wavering (for he is faithful that promised) (Heb. 10:23).

DAD

CHAPTER THIRTEEN

THE BRIDGE BUILDER

WILL ALLEN DROMGOOLE

THE FOLLOWING POEM SHOULD
STRIKE A CHORD IN THE HEART OF
EVERY DAD. WHAT DOES THE BRIDGE
IN THIS OLD CHESTNUT SYMBOLIZE?
SURELY IT REPRESENTS THE GOSPEL
MESSAGE — THE ONLY WAY TO GET
TO THE "OTHER SIDE" OF LIFE, AND
THAT IS THROUGH SALVATION, BY
REPENTING OF OUR SINS AND

TRUSTING FULLY IN THE
SAVING GRACE OF OUR SAVIOR,
WHO BUILT THAT FIRST BRIDGE
FOR EACH ONE OF US WITH ONLY
THREE NAILS AND TWO PIECES
OF WOOD. IT'S UP TO FATHERS
TO PASS THE TORCH ON TO
THEIR OWN CHILDREN.
DAD, HAVE YOU BUILT THAT BRIDGE?

Bear ye one another's burdens, and so fulfill the law of Christ (Gal. 6:2).

DAD

An old man, going a lone highway,

Came, at the evening, cold and gray,

To a chasm, vast, and deep, and wide,

Through which was flowing a sullen tide.

The old man crossed in the twilight dim;

The sullen stream had no fears for him;

But he turned, when safe on the other side,

And built a bridge to span the tide.

"Old man," said a fellow pilgrim, near,

"You are wasting strength with building here;

Your journey will end with the ending day;

You never again must pass this way;

You have crossed the chasm, deep and wide —

Why build you the bridge at the eventide?"

The builder lifted his old gray head:

"Good friend, in the path I have come," he said,

"There followeth after me today

A youth, whose feet must pass this way.

This chasm, that has been naught to me,

To that fair-haired youth may a pitfall be.

He, too, must cross in the twilight dim;

Good friend, I am building the bridge for him."

Bear ye one another's burdens, and so fulfill the law of Christ (Gal. 6:2).

DAD

AND HE SHALL TURN THE
HEARTS OF THE FATHERS
TO THEIR CHILDREN,
AND THE HEARTS
OF THE CHILDREN
TO THEIR FATHERS
(MAL. 4:6).

ENDNOTES

1. Robert Strand, *Moments for Fathers* (Green Forest, AR: New Leaf Press, 1994).

2. "A New Voice" by Art Stricklin, taken from *Sports Spectrum*, a Christian sports magazine. Used by permission. For subscription information call 1-800-283-8333.

3. "The Good Provider" by James Lloyd. Reprinted with permission from *Guideposts* magazine (February 2002), copyright © 2001 by Guideposts, Carmel, New York 10512.